Harry Potter™

MAGICAL

PLACES & CHARACTERS

COLORING BOOK

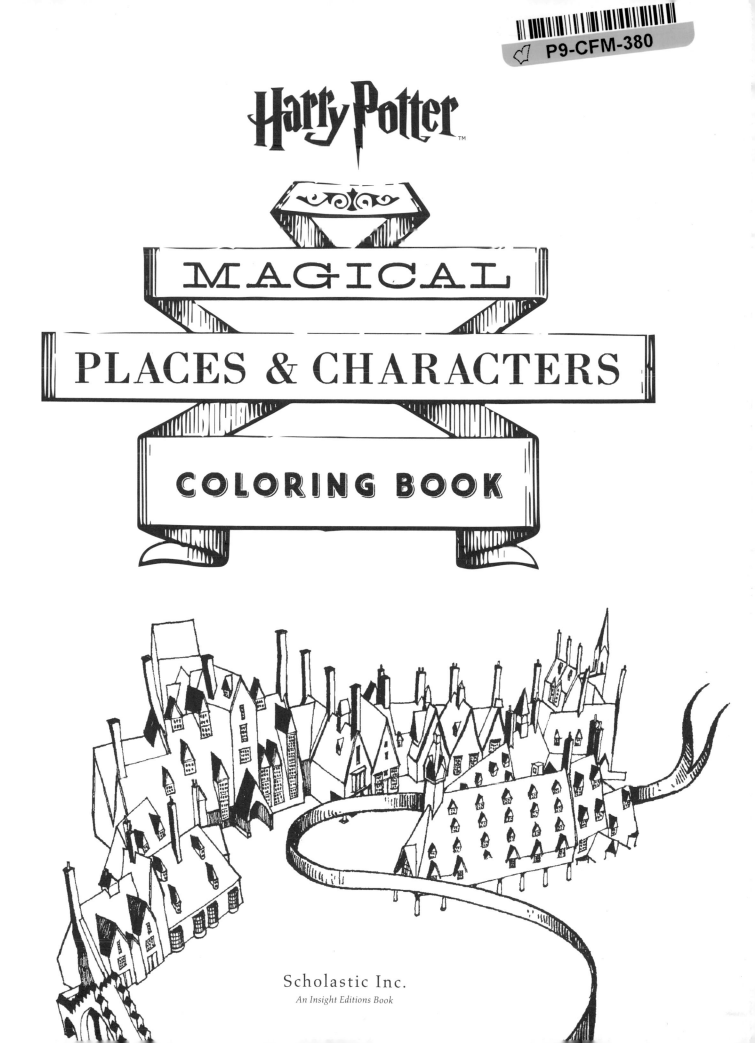

Scholastic Inc.

An Insight Editions Book

The world we journey through in the Harry Potter films is magical and extraordinary. From a bank run by goblins to a castle filled with staircases that move, we are continually taken to new and incredible places. We follow a young boy who has discovered a world he never knew existed and we encounter there a thrilling cast of wizards, witches— and so much more. The pages that follow are an invitation to relive the magic of the Harry Potter films and bring your own vibrant colors to the wizarding world outlined here in black and white.

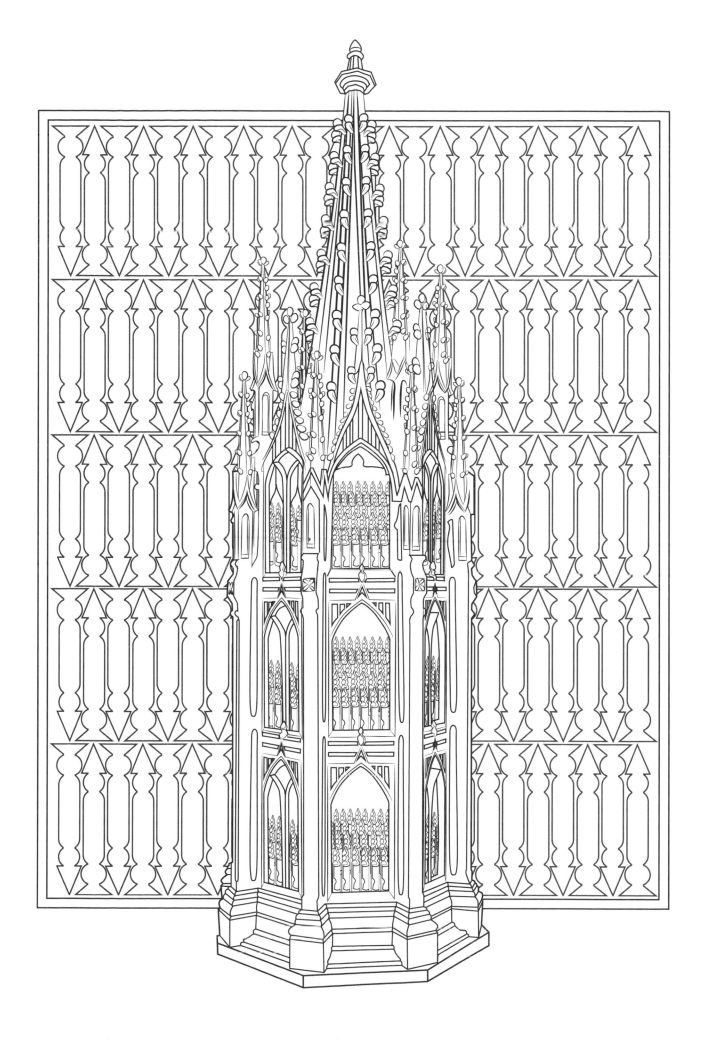

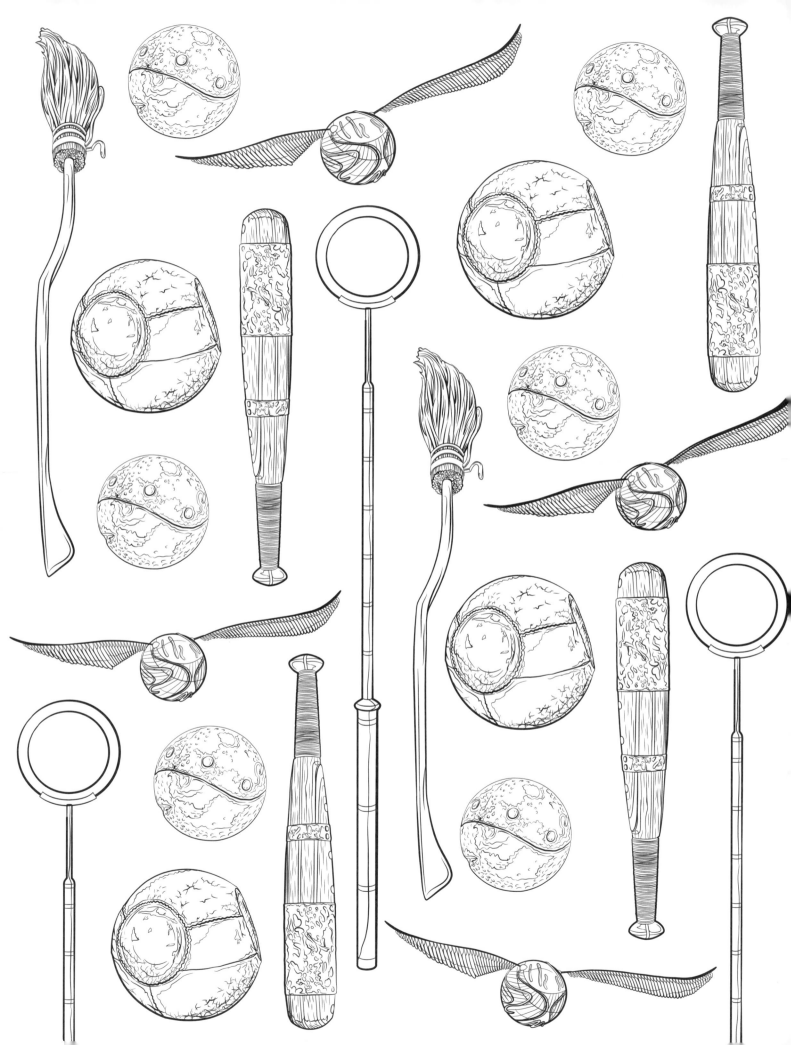

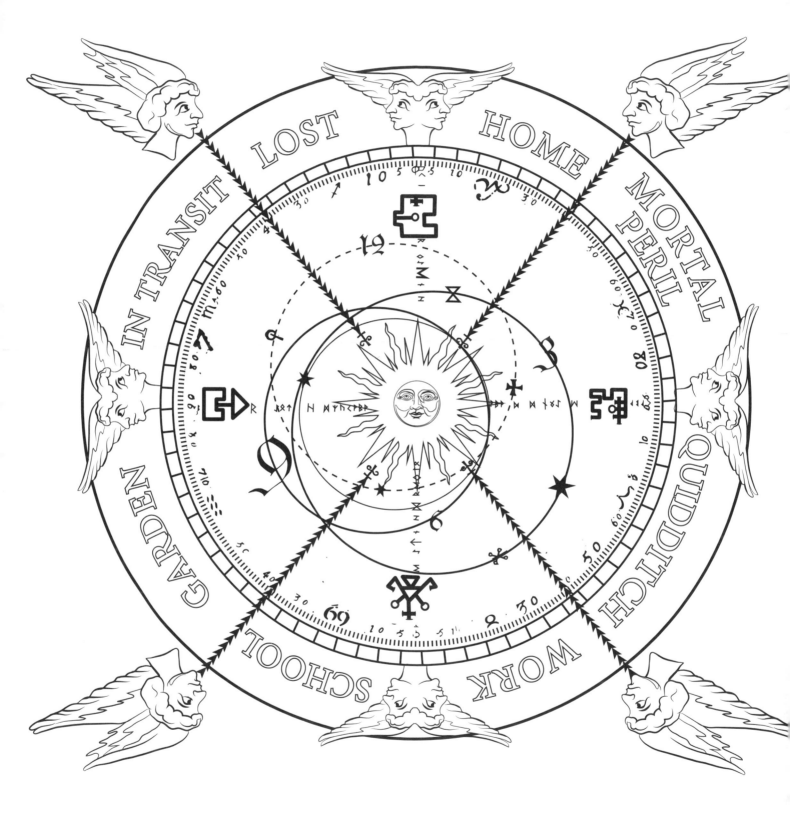

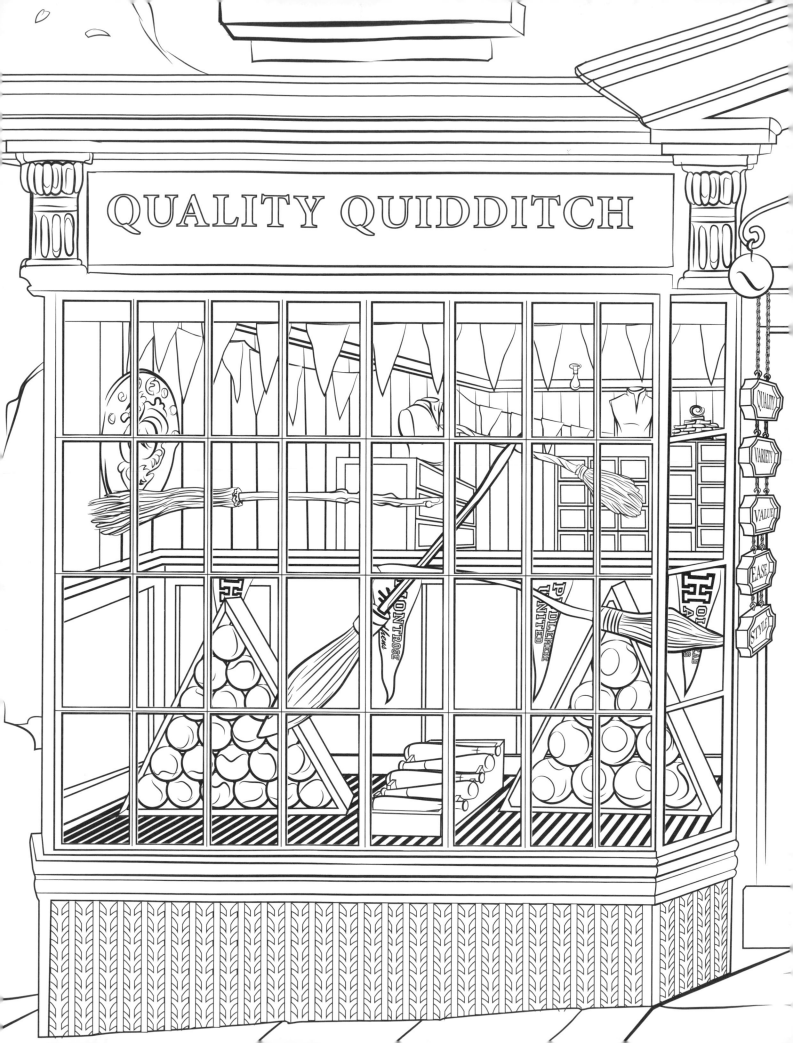

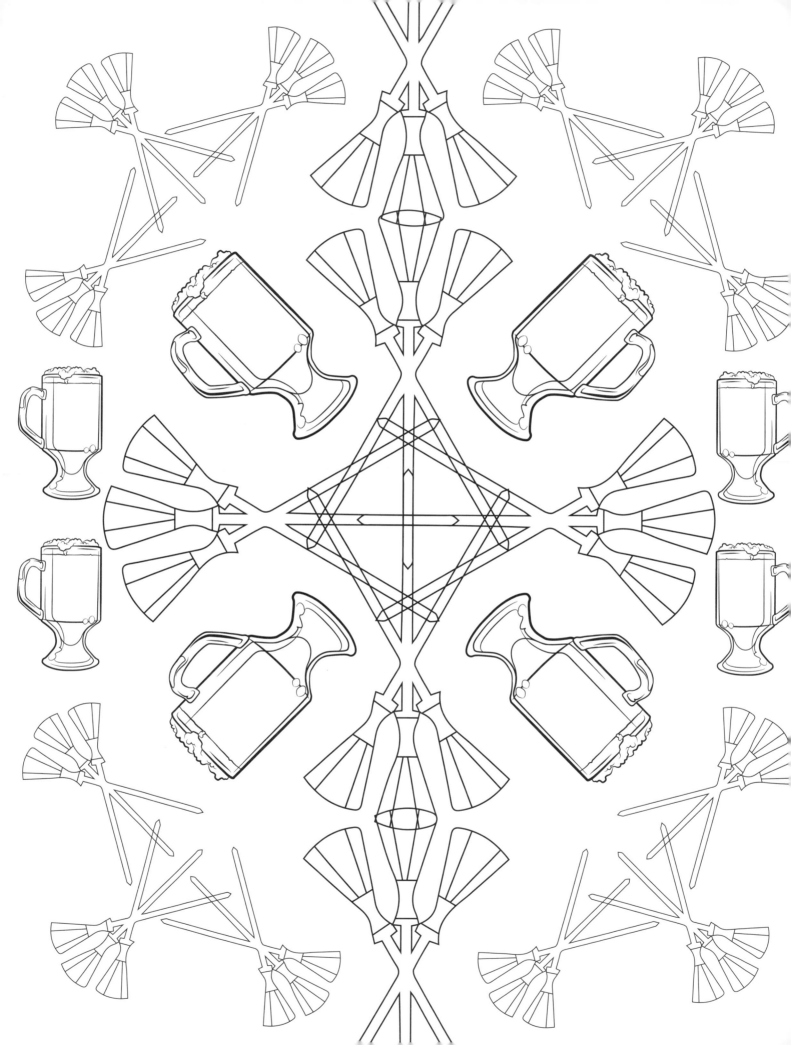

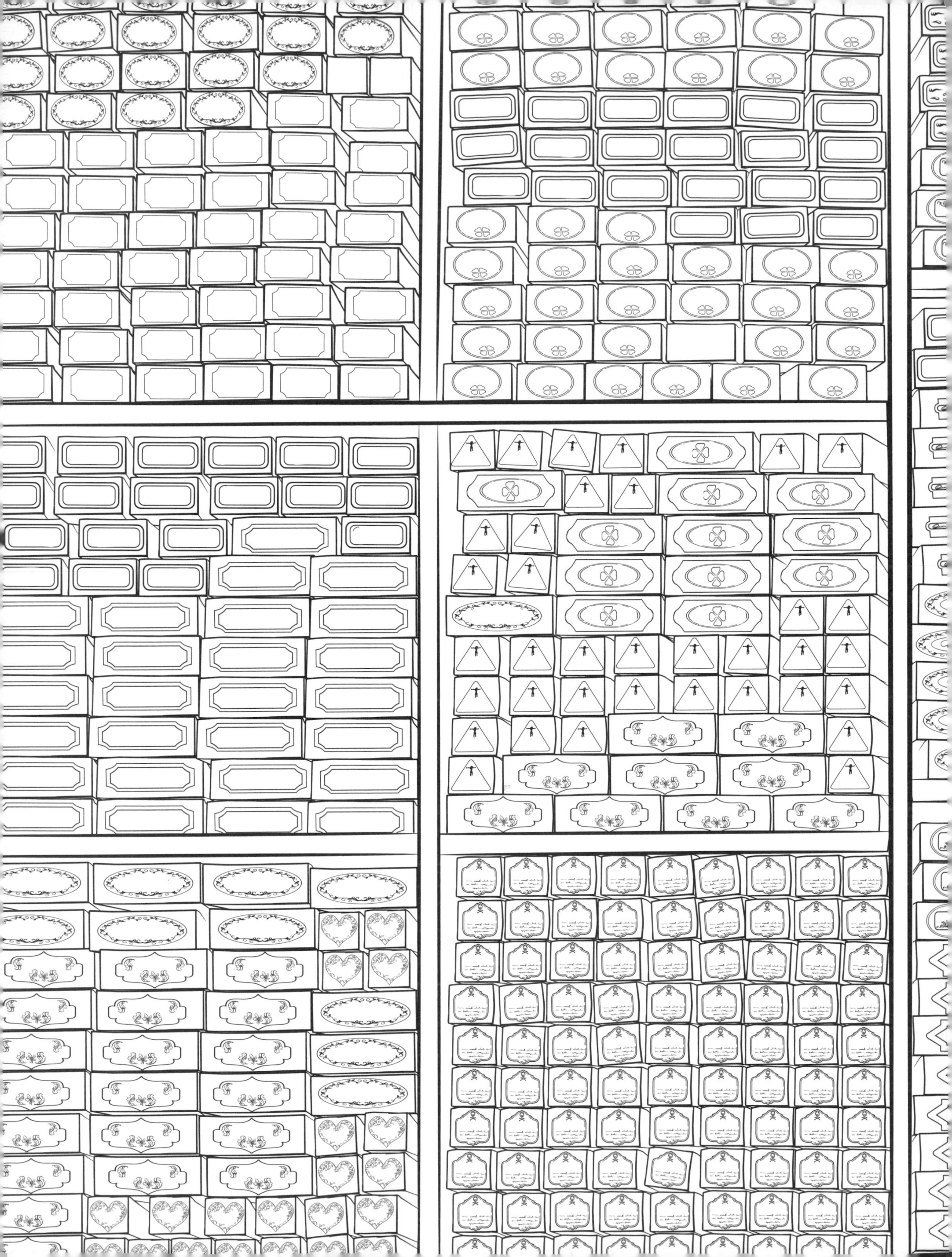

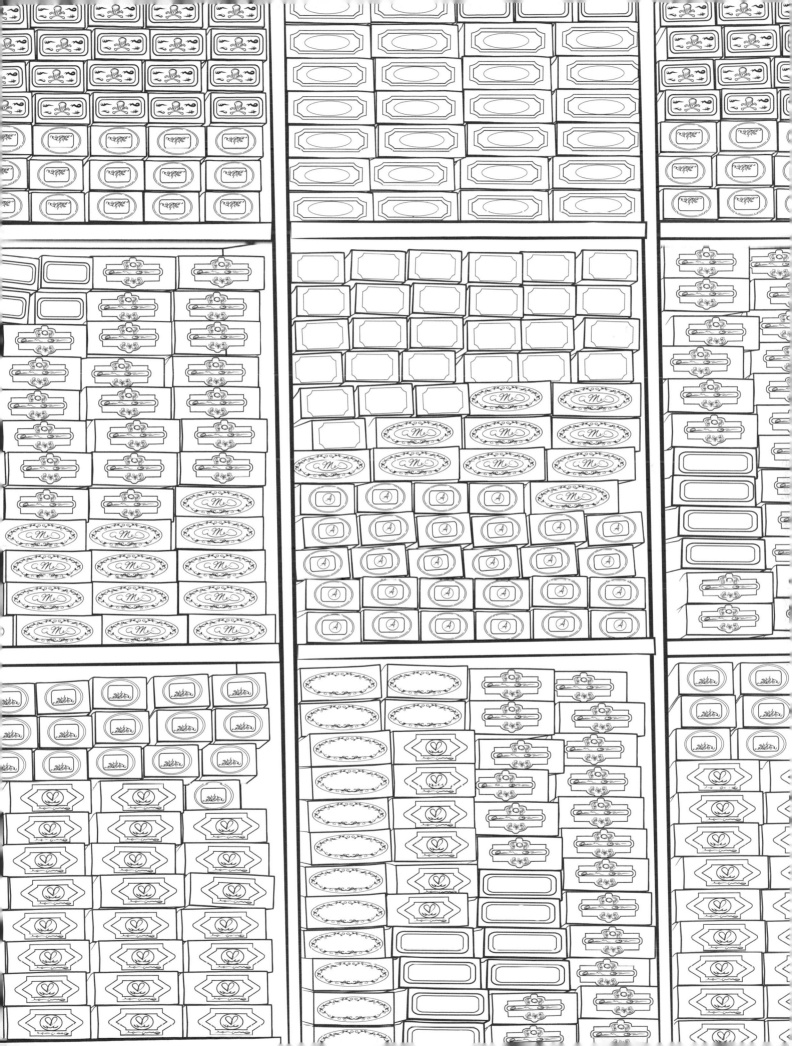

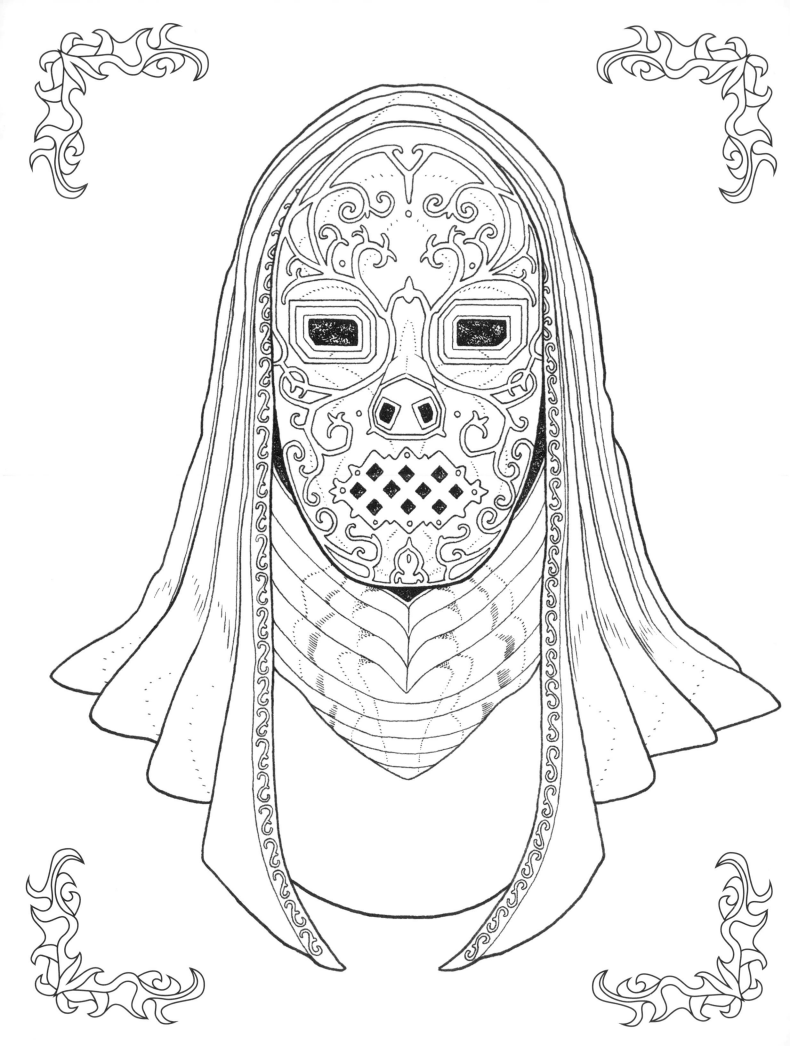

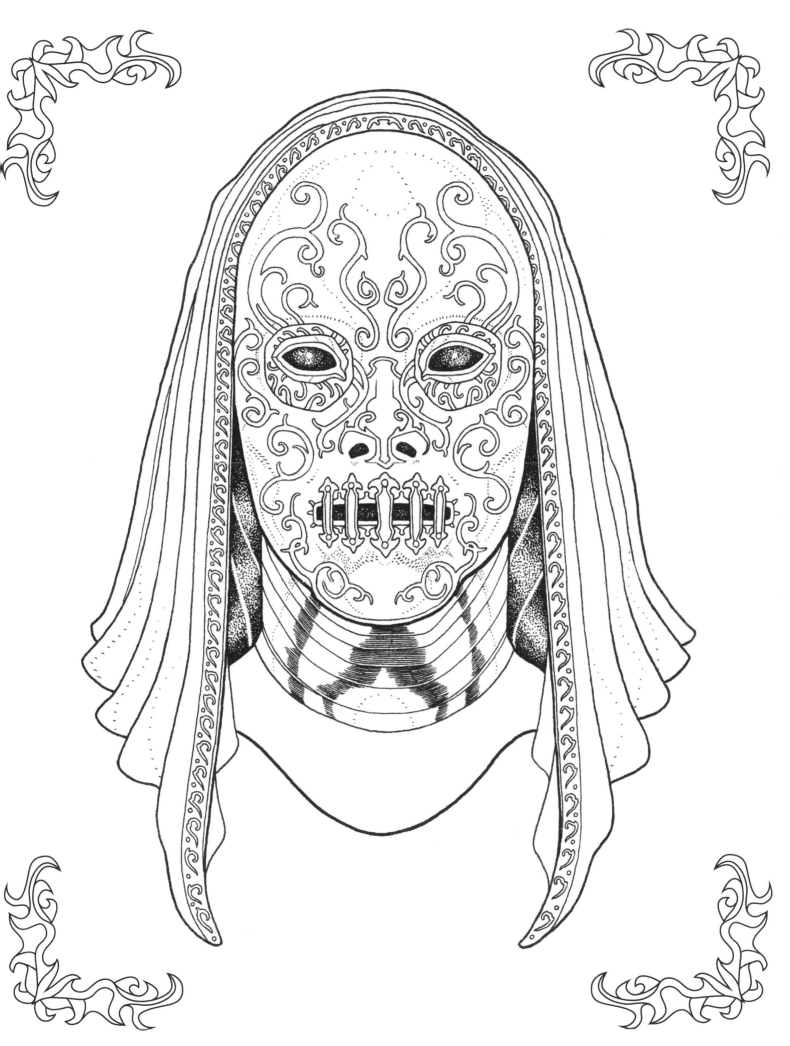

ART CREDITS:
Hogwarts castle, herbology classroom, library, Burrow, and escape
from Gringotts concept art by Andrew Williamson. Prefect's bathroom
window, Weasleys' Wizard Wheezes storefront, and Quidditch pitch
concept art by Adam Brockbank. Death Eater masks by Rob Bliss.

Produced by

INSIGHT
EDITIONS
PO Box 3088
San Rafael, CA 94912

www.insighteditions.com

PUBLISHER: Raoul Goff
ART DIRECTOR: Chrissy Kwasnik
COVER DESIGN & LAYOUT: Jenelle Wagner
EXECUTIVE EDITOR: Vanessa Lopez
PROJECT EDITOR: Greg Solano
PRODUCTION EDITOR: Rachel Anderson
PRODUCTION MANAGER: Blake Mitchum
JUNIOR PRODUCTION MANAGER: Alix Nicholaeff
PRODUCTION COORDINATOR: Leeana Diaz

INSIGHT EDITIONS would like to thank Victoria Selover,
Elaine Piechowski, and Melanie Swartz.

ILLUSTRATIONS BY Adam Raiti, Robin F. Williams, Maxime Lebrun,
Dee Pei, Frans Boukas, Britt Wilson, and Manuel Martinez.

ROOTS of PEACE ⊙ REPLANTED PAPER

Insight Editions, in association with Roots of Peace, will plant two trees for each tree
used in the manufacturing of this book. Roots of Peace is an internationally renowned
humanitarian organization dedicated to eradicating land mines worldwide and
converting war-torn lands into productive farms and wildlife habitats. Roots of Peace
will plant two million fruit and nut trees in Afghanistan and provide farmers there
with the skills and support necessary for sustainable land use.

Manufactured in the United States by Insight Editions

10 9 8 7 6 5 4 3 2 1